NATIONAL GEOGRAPHIC
Ladde
AMAZING PLANTS

GENRE Myth

Read to find out how Padma defeated the witch.

THE KING'S TREE

RETOLD BY ELIZABETH GILBERT

ILLUSTRATED BY KARLA DIAZ CASTRO

DURING THE WEEKS FOLLOWING HER WEDDING, PADMA ADJUSTED TO LIFE AT THE PALACE. SHE AND THE KING WERE THE HAPPIEST COUPLE IN ALL THE LAND.
DREADED WITCH, HOWEVER, WAS DISPLEASED WITH THEIR JOY. IT WASN'T LONG BEFORE THE WITCH BEGAN WORKING HARD TO RUIN PADMA'S HAPPINESS.
OUCH!
YOUR JOY WILL NOT LAST. EVEN NOW, YOUR KING THINKS YOU ARE LESS BEAUTIFUL THAN YESTERDAY!
PADMA MADE A PLAN. IT SADDENED HER BECAUSE SHE WOULD HAVE TO GIVE UP HER LIFE WITH THE KING, BUT IT WAS THE ONLY WAY SHE COULD DEFEAT DREADED WITCH.

IN THE MIDDLE OF THE NIGHT, PADMA WHISPERED GOODBYE TO HER SLEEPING HUSBAND . . .
AND SNEAKED OUT TO THE PEACEFUL WATER GARDEN ON THE PALACE GROUNDS.
PADMA PLUNGED INTO THE SHALLOW POOL IN THE GARDEN AND CHANGED INTO A LOTUS FLOWER.
THE NEXT MORNING, THE KING AWOKE WITH A SUSPICION THAT SOMETHING WAS TERRIBLY WRONG. HE DECIDED HE MUST FIND PADMA RIGHT AWAY.

THE KING COMMANDED EVERYONE TO SEARCH THE PALACE AND ITS SURROUNDINGS, BUT PADMA WAS NOWHERE TO BE FOUND.
AFTER ALMOST GIVING UP HOPE, THE KING FOUND HIMSELF AT THE WATER GARDEN BEHIND THE PALACE. THERE HE SAW THE LOTUS FLOWER IN ITS WATERY **HABITAT.**
FROM WHERE CAME THIS BEAUTIFUL FLOWER? IT BRINGS ME STRANGE JOY, AS IF I WERE SEEING PADMA HERSELF, THOUGH IT BE JUST A FLOWER.
I SHALL VISIT ITS LOVELY PETALS EVERY DAY!
I MUST DESTROY THAT UGLY FLOWER!
AFTER THE KING HAD GONE, DREADED WITCH CAST A SPELL ON THE POOL, DRAINING ITS WATER.
THEN SHE CAST ANOTHER SPELL, WHICH CAUSED THE FLOWER TO BURST INTO FLAMES, LEAVING ONLY ASHES.

LATER THAT NIGHT . . .
A TINY PLANT SPROUTED FROM THE FLOWER'S ASHES.
THE SPROUT UNCURLED AND GREW TALLER AND TALLER.
FROM THE LOTUS ASHES GREW THE FIRST MANGO TREE, **BLOOMING** WITH HUNDREDS OF FLOWERS.
YESTERDAY, THIS POOL WAS FULL OF WATER, AND WITHIN IT BLOOMED ONE BEAUTIFUL LOTUS FLOWER.
IN THIS CHANGED HABITAT STANDS A KIND OF TREE I'VE NEVER SEEN IN ALL THE LAND. YET THE TREE HAS **ADAPTATIONS** THAT MAKE IT WONDERFULLY SUITED TO THIS PLACE.
IT HAS NOT ONE FLOWER, BUT HUNDREDS!
ONE DAY, WHEN THE KING VISITED THE MANGO TREE, HE NOTICED A MYSTERIOUS FRUIT HAD BEGUN TO GROW FROM ITS BRANCHES.

Check In What plants did Padma change into?

GENRE Science Article

Read to find out about some of Earth's most extreme plants.

Extreme Plants

by Jennifer Boudart

Plants have taken root in almost every kind of **habitat** on Earth. They grow down low, in ponds and marshes. They grow up high, along mountain ridges. Plants even grow in harsh habitats, such as burning deserts and freezing tundra. Plants have **adaptations** that help them survive in their environment. The way they look and grow helps them survive. Plants take many forms, from towering trees to tiny bits of green. The following plants have taken adaptation to extremes.

The Biggest Bloomer!

The rafflesia is a rare jungle plant found in Southeast Asia. The rafflesia produces just one flower, but it's a whopper. This flower grows up to 1 meter (about 3 feet) across and weighs up to 7 kilograms (15 pounds). The **bloom** actually smells awful—just like rotting meat! The stench attracts flies that feed on dead animals. The flies pick up pollen as they crawl on the flower. When they buzz to another stinky bloom, they spread the pollen to another plant. Pollen must be transferred between plants for the plants to reproduce.

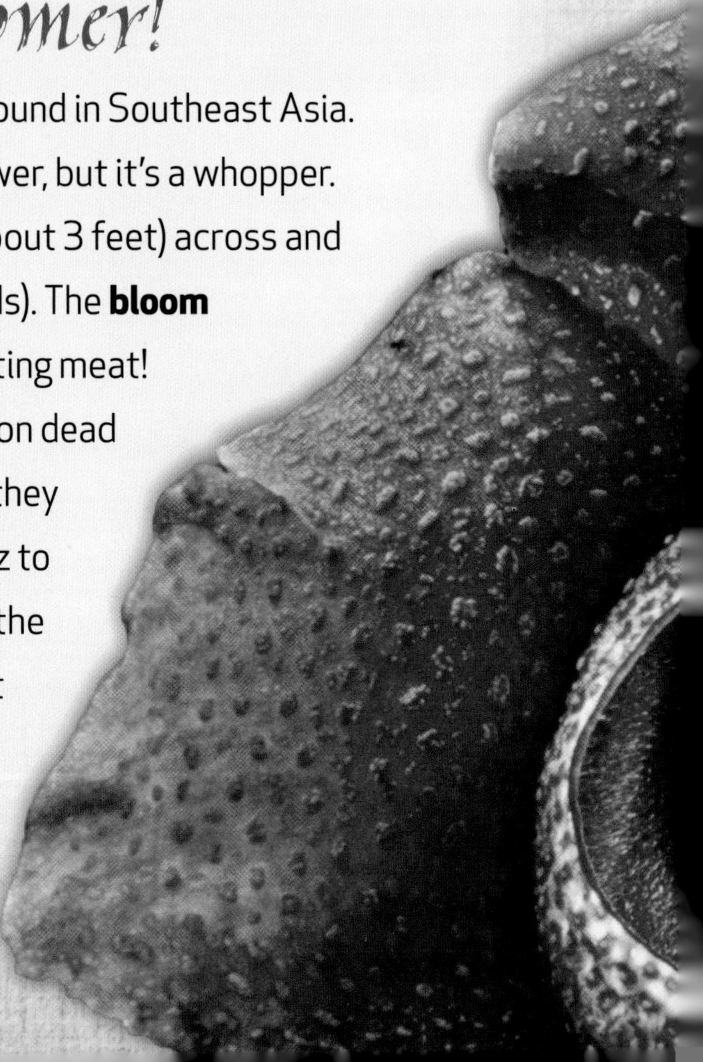

The rafflesia's bloom is the largest in the world.

A Green Giant!

The giant sequoia truly lives up to its name. This tree is more massive, or has more bulk, than any other plant **species** on Earth. That earns it the title of biggest plant. The giant sequoia's trunk accounts for most of its mass. The trunk on a full-grown tree typically measures more than 6 meters (20 feet) across. Giant sequoias are tall, too. They often stand 76 meters (about 250 feet) tall. A few tower more than 93 meters (305 feet). That's taller than the Statue of Liberty!

To see the giant sequoias, you have to visit the Sierra Nevada in eastern California.

Giant sequoias can live a very long time. Many have survived more than 3,000 years. What adaptations help giant sequoias live so long? Their bark is resistant to disease. Also, giant sequoias can grow new bark quickly to cover burns caused by forest fires. When a fully grown giant sequoia dies, it's typically because the tree fell over after the soil became unstable.

The most massive giant sequoia is named the General Sherman Tree. This tree stands about 84 meters (275 feet) tall and weighs 5.6 million kilograms (12 million pounds). Its trunk measures 11 meters (35 feet) across! If the General Sherman were cut for lumber, it would supply enough wood to build 40 houses. Luckily the General Sherman is protected by laws that make it illegal to cut down giant sequoias.

This is King Clone, the oldest known creosote bush. It forms a ring about 14 meters (45 feet) across. Scientists think King Clone first sprouted from a seed 13,700 years ago!

Blast from the Past!

The creosote bush grows in the deserts of North America. It's a super survivor. In fact, creosote bushes are among the longest-living plants on Earth. A creosote bush appears as a ring of bushes growing around an empty center. Each bush in the ring actually comes from the same parent plant, which once grew inside the circle. And each bush is an exact copy of that parent plant. This is the secret to the creosote bush's long life.

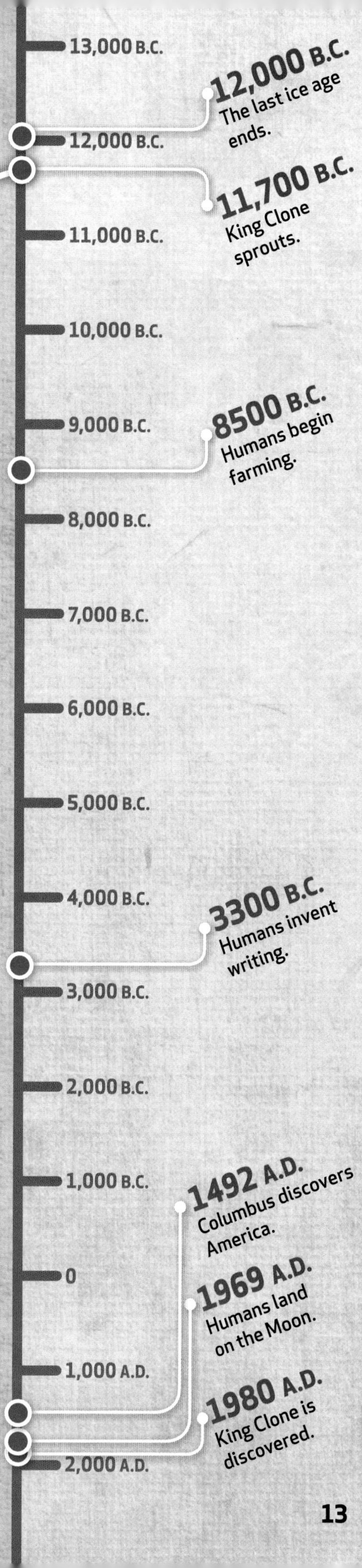

A single creosote bush can live 200 years. During that time, the bush sends out shoots in all directions. Each shoot grows into a new, identical bush. That bush, in turn, produces new copies of itself. Over time, the original plant dies, leaving an ever-expanding ring of "daughter" plants behind. The parent plant "lives on" because it has made exact copies of itself. In this way, some creosote bushes have stuck around for thousands of years.

A Turbo Grower!

Bamboo thrives in the warm, wet climates of East and Southeast Asia. Some species of bamboo may be the fastest-growing plants on Earth.

Bamboos are grasses, but they look more like trees because of their woody stem and leafy branches. And, like trees, some grow very tall. A few species of bamboo reach 40 meters (about 130 feet) or more. Unlike trees, however, bamboo can grow at incredible speeds in the right environment. The speediest ones may sprout up 60 centimeters (about 2 feet) in one day. That's 2.5 centimeters (1 inch) per hour. Imagine if the grass in people's lawns grew that fast!

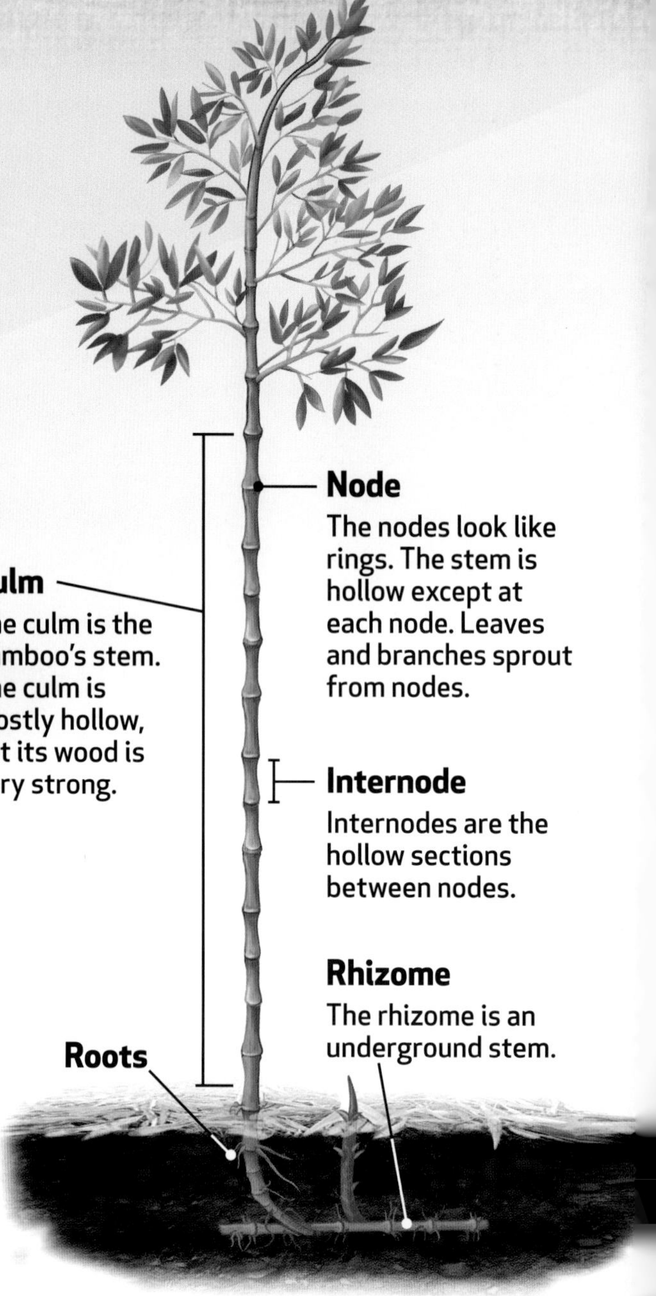

People use bamboo in thousands of ways. The seeds and shoots can be eaten. Its sturdy wood can be used to make furniture, musical instruments, and homes. How are these people using bamboo?

A bamboo forest near Kyoto, Japan

A Microgreen!

Watermeal is the world's smallest flowering plant species. Imagine holding a small grain of sand in your palm—that's how little a watermeal is. Lacking roots and stems, its tiny size and rounded form are adaptations that help it float in large numbers on lakes, ponds, marshes, and streams. One watermeal plant is less than a millimeter long and weighs about as much as a few grains of salt. A dozen of the plant's blooms could fit on the head of a pin!

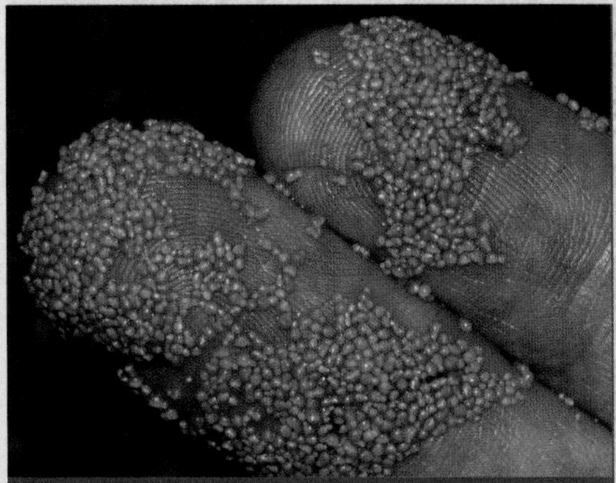

A person's fingers show how tiny watermeal plants are.

A giant Amazon water lily can easily support 23 kilograms (50 pounds).

A Leaf Beyond Belief!

Do you think only frogs can float on lily pads? Think again! A giant Amazon water lily is so large it can support the weight of people without sinking. Its leaves stretch 2.5 meters (8 feet) across. This plant's adaptations help keep it afloat. The weight of its wide, flat leaves is spread out, causing the leaves to float. Air-filled veins also help make the leaves buoyant. Spines cover the underside of each leaf to protect it from hungry fish. Notches along the edges help extra water drain off, so the leaf doesn't fill and sink.

This giant Amazon water lily can hold three people.

It's clear some plant species have developed extreme adaptations to survive. Do any extreme plants grow where you live?

Check In Which extreme plants can live for longer than 3,000 years?

GENRE Play

Read to find out what plants the students find.

The Plant Hunt

by Renee Biermann
illustrated by C. B. Canga

NARRATOR

MRS. BLANKENSHIP
female teacher

INTRODUCTION

[**SETTING** *The play takes place at City Botanical Gardens.* NARRATOR *enters and speaks to the audience.*]

NARRATOR: Welcome to City Botanical Gardens! Mrs. Blankenship has brought a special group of students to this indoor **habitat** for a scavenger hunt. She has given them a Scavenger Hunt Notebook, a measuring tape, and gardening gloves. They are going to hunt for five unusual plants. How will they locate these mysterious plants? And what will they discover at the end of the hunt? Let's find out!

ACT 1, SCENE 1

[**SETTING** *Near the entrance of City Botanical Gardens.* MADDIE, JIN, ANTWON, NOAH, PIPPA, *and* ANNABELLE *are listening to* MRS. BLANKENSHIP.]

MRS. BLANKENSHIP: Look carefully at your Scavenger Hunt Notebook. Use it as much as possible. Be sure to wear your gardening gloves because some plants are poisonous. Have fun! I'll see you at the end for a *big surprise*!

[MRS. BLANKENSHIP *exits. Students look excited about the big surprise.*]

NOAH: [*holds up Scavenger Hunt Notebook*] Let's look at the notebook together. [*flips through pages and shows group*] There is one page for each plant. We have to mark "yes" or "no" for the plant **characteristics.** We also have to list the plant name. There is room for our comments, too.

PIPPA: Where do we begin?

ANTWON: [*pulls piece of folded paper out of pocket*] Mrs. Blankenship gave me this piece of paper when we came in. She told me not to look at it until the hunt started. Maybe it will help.

JIN: Will you read it to us?

ANTWON: It says, "I have a trunk. I stand tall. I'm named after one of the biggest animals of all."

ANNABELLE: [*confused*] That sounds like an elephant! [*excited*] Wait! I saw a big plant that had leaves like elephant ears when we came in.

MADDIE: Let's start there!

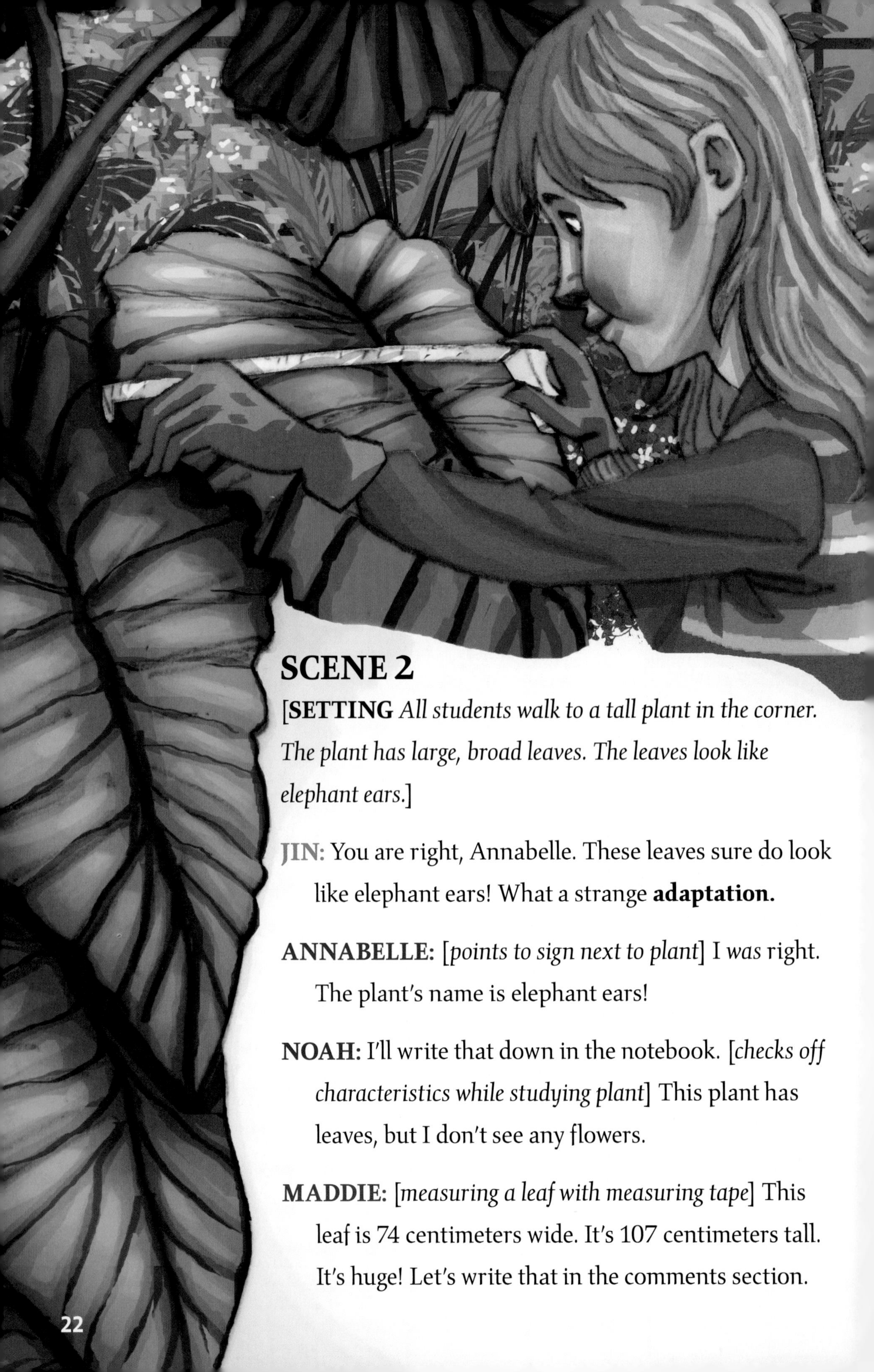

SCENE 2

[**SETTING** *All students walk to a tall plant in the corner. The plant has large, broad leaves. The leaves look like elephant ears.*]

JIN: You are right, Annabelle. These leaves sure do look like elephant ears! What a strange **adaptation.**

ANNABELLE: [*points to sign next to plant*] I *was* right. The plant's name is elephant ears!

NOAH: I'll write that down in the notebook. [*checks off characteristics while studying plant*] This plant has leaves, but I don't see any flowers.

MADDIE: [*measuring a leaf with measuring tape*] This leaf is 74 centimeters wide. It's 107 centimeters tall. It's huge! Let's write that in the comments section.

JIN: No flowers are **blooming** on this plant. It doesn't have vines or a scent. Check "no" for those characteristics.

PIPPA: We figured out this plant quickly. But where do we go next? Antwon, did Mrs. Blankenship give you any other clues?

ANTWON: [*holds up clue*] No, this is the only one.

ANNABELLE: Look! [*points to bottom of plant*] There is a new piece of paper!

NOAH: [*reads paper aloud*] "I'm tiny as can be. I'm an itty bitty tree!"

MADDIE: Let's go look for the new plant!

SCENE 3

[**SETTING** *Students are walking along the pathway.*]

PIPPA: [*thinking hard*] There are a bunch of trees in this habitat. Which one is the clue talking about?

JIN: [*points to nearby plant*] That plant over there looks like a tiny tree.

NOAH: I think you found it! This one is called a bonsai tree. [*writes name in notebook*]

PIPPA: The sign says this plant comes from Japan.

MADDIE: That's amazing! It also has small, pink flowers. [*sniffs*] They have a light scent. [*measures plant*] This plant is only 13 centimeters tall.

[NOAH *records characteristics in notebook.*]

ANNABELLE: It really does look like a tiny tree. We should write that in the comments section.

NOAH: [*writing*] No problem!

[JIN *reaches down. He pulls a piece of paper from under the plant's pot.*]

JIN: I found the new clue! "We do not sit on the ground. Look up high and think of *sound.*"

[*Students go to search for next plant.*]

SCENE 4

[**SETTING** *Students are looking at plants that are hanging from the ceiling.*]

NOAH: What kind of musical instruments do we know?

JIN: There's the flute, the saxophone, the violin, the guitar…

ANTWON: [*stops to read a plant name*] I found it! It's called angel's trumpet!

ANNABELLE: Those flowers do look kind of like trumpets. They are beautiful.

MADDIE: [*stretches to measure*] Wow—this plant is 2 meters tall! [*sniffs flowers*] The flowers smell great!

PIPPA: Be careful, Maddie. The sign says this plant is poisonous.

JIN: I'm really happy Mrs. Blankenship gave us these gloves!

[*All students nod and agree with* JIN.]

NOAH: I wrote down the information we need. Who has the next clue?

ANNABELLE: [*pulls clue out of middle of plant*] Here it is! It says: "I make many things taste yummy. Look up high where it's sunny."

ANTWON: [*excited*] I know that one right away! It's a vanilla orchid!

PIPPA: [*doubtful*] How do you know that?

ANTWON: My aunt grows orchids. She told me about the vanilla one. It's a huge vine. [*points to distance*] There it is!

[*Students walk to huge vine growing up a post.*]

PIPPA: I'm sorry I didn't believe you, Antwon. This sign says vanilla orchid. It says all of the vanilla in the world comes from these plants. The sign says they're originally from present-day Mexico.

NOAH: I'm going to write that along with our information. [*begins writing*]

MADDIE: [*looks worried*] Oh, no! I'm never going to be able to measure it. It's so high!

JIN: Let's **estimate** the height. I'm sure Mrs. Blankenship will understand. She wouldn't want us to climb up there!

ANNABELLE: I would estimate that it's about 5 meters tall.

[*Students nod in agreement.* NOAH *records information.*]

PIPPA: [*sniffs and makes a face*] Do you guys smell something? It stinks!

NOAH: [*sniffs orchid*] It's not this plant. This plant has a sweet scent. [*writes information in notebook*] It must be coming from something else.

JIN: [*pulls out piece of paper that is tucked in vine and reads it*] I think the final clue will help us. Listen to this: "Use your nose to find me. I don't smell like other lilies."

ANTWON: Follow that stinky scent!

SCENE 5

[**SETTING** *Students come around a corner.* MRS. BLANKENSHIP *is standing next to a gigantic plant. She is holding her nose.* NARRATOR *enters and addresses audience.*]

NARRATOR: The students are almost finished with the Scavenger Hunt. They have recorded important information about each plant they found. Now, they are ready to find the big surprise—and boy, is it BIG!

MRS. BLANKENSHIP: Surprise! You made it!

[*Students make faces at stinky odor.*]

JIN: What is that?

MADDIE: [*quickly measuring*] It's 1.2 meters tall!

[NOAH *records information in the notebook.*]

MRS. BLANKENSHIP: [*laughing*] This plant is called the voodoo lily. It only blooms once a year. When it blooms, it smells like something is rotting! The scent attracts pollinators to help the plant reproduce.

NOAH: [*makes uncomfortable sound*] That's for sure. It smells awful!

ANNABELLE: [*interested*] I don't care that it smells bad. It's amazing! And it sure is a *big surprise.*

[*Students all nod in agreement.*]

MRS. BLANKENSHIP: [*happy*] I hope you had a good time today. You did a great job of identifying all of the plants. Would you like to come here again sometime?

[*Students all say "yes." They cheer.*]

Check In Which plant does vanilla come from?

Discuss Characters, Stories, and Main Ideas

1. What do you think connects the three pieces that you read in this book? What makes you think that?

2. Choose an illustration in "The King's Tree." What additional information does it give about the characters or the setting?

3. What is the main idea of "Extreme Plants"? Explain how you think each plant's most extreme feature might be useful to it.

4. In "The Plant Hunt," what event usually leads to the start of a new scene?

5. What do you still wonder about plants? What would be some good ways to find more information?